CAT CHAT

Judy Gardiner

Illustrations

Tony Hatt

FREDERICK MULLER LIMITED
LONDON

First published in Great Britain 1978
by Frederick Muller Limited, London, NW2 6LE

ISBN 0 584 10453 7

British Library Cataloguing in Publication Data

Gardiner, Judy
Cat chat.
1. Cats — Anecdotes, facetiae, satire etc.
I. Title
636.8'08'30207 SF447

ISBN 0—584—10453—7

Typeset by Texet, Leighton Buzzard, Bedfordshire and Printed in Great Britain by Billing & Sons Ltd., Guildford, London and Worcester.

Contents

For Angela
from both of us.

Preface

ats can do almost anything. They can hear sounds up to 30,000 to 45,000 cycles per second and can see in the dark seven times better than we can. They can also swim and climb trees; turn in mid-air and land on their feet, understand Stockhausen and sleep on a gatepost. Some of the women ones can knit, but not very well.

Cats can do almost anything, but some things they prefer not to do simply because it doesn't interest them. Under this heading comes closing doors and wiping their feet. One of the things they are particularly good at is watching. They will spend hours watching anything from snowflakes to Tom and Jerry, and they can often be seen watching human beings with a sweet, musing expression.

I've been watching cats for over fifty years, and the pastime never palls. Sometimes I think I know a lot about them, (almost enough to write a large and officious kind of *Principia Catica*), then I meet another cat threading its way through another set of railings and the delight is so new and surprising that I might never have seen one before.

So I'm not apologising for the size of this book. I'm just explaining.

Judy Gardiner

1

Cooking for Cats

ats are dainty feeders, as it said in the sixpenny cat book of my youth, and that's only one way of describing the most gastronomically capricious creature of all time. (Silkworms could probably be described as capricious for only eating mulberry leaves, but they are at least consistent.) Cats however, are connoisseurs, and eat not merely to keep body and soul together, but for aesthetic reasons as well. Which is why they don't gollop like dogs, and why they always eat with their eyes closed.

Although cats are hunting creatures, a diet of vermin and birds leads sooner or later to intestinal parasites; part of the developing process of tape worms takes place within rats and mice, and once established inside a cat are very difficult to eradicate entirely. A kitchen-fed cat will hunt vermin with equal zest, and if a real mouse is not available then a toy one will do almost as well. Only don't call it *playing*; and above all don't laugh at all the hiding, peering, pouncing and patting. Just applaud the skill and thank God that you're not three inches high. It must be terrible to be patted to death.

A common reason for cats declining to eat what they're given is simply that it's cold. Carnivores are accustomed to dine on food that is at blood-heat so try warming the reject in a saucepan, and if the smell appalls you, jam the lid down hard. But better still, start cooking properly for your cat — it takes very little time and money once you get the hang of it — and cats are frequently more appreciative of culinary effort than the average family.

You start by finding a butcher or supermarket that stocks good pet meat. This consists of frozen blocks or rolls of minced offal and scraps of boneless meat. Some of it can be rather coarse and fat but it's always very very cheap. Simmer it in water until just cooked through, then remove it to a basin with a slotted spoon and allow any fat to settle in a hard crust on top of the gravy in the pan. Give the fat to the birds, keep the gravy in a jug and warm it before pouring it over the meat and serving it.

This is Cats' Basic Nosh, and is the gateway to a thousand gastronomic delights, such as:

RAGOÛT A LA BONNE CHATTE

For this you will need one tablespoonful of pet meat which has been enriched by the addition of half a beef stock cube to the cooking water, half a small tin of cat food, and a handful of corn flakes.

Warm the pet meat in its gravy, blend in the tinned meat and stir in the corn flakes, but leave some to stay crisp and crunchy on top. This will fill one large cat or three medium kittens.

Another dish easily concocted from Cats' Basic is:

KATERINA'S BOLOGNESE

This was in fact the favourite dish of a Soho-dwelling

cat back in the fifties who walked with peerless hauteur because her great-great-great grandmother had once been stroked by Dylan Thomas in a pub.

For Katerina's Bolognese cut out the corn flakes and substitute pasta, (the remains of yesterday's rice pudding would be particularly good), and then just before serving grate a little bit of cheese on top.

Never be afraid to blend fish with meat; the odd sardine or even a little sardine juice mingled with the Basic will (in the words of the cat book) often be well tolerated, and a spoonful of any tinned cat food added to the cooked meat and gravy will do a lot to banish monotony. Cats are imaginative creatures and eating the same thing every day can get on their nerves.

Conversely, I once knew a cat called Nellie who only ate Marmite sandwiches. She belonged to a doting lady in Broadstairs who always cut the crusts off and people used to say 'How on earth can Nellie keep fit on such a crazy diet?'

They forgot that Marmite is rich in the B vitamins and that both butter and bread are important sources of energy, and when you allow for Nellie's conviction that Marmite sandwiches were the sole means of keeping breath within her body, it's not all that surprising that she throve. It would have been very taxing however, supposing she had had to explain her dietry phobia to a new owner.

Almost all cats enjoy weak Marmite or Bovril in the form of a *tisane*, finding that it restores the tissues and calms the nerves. And for a convalescent cat there is nothing to beat a saucerful of:

CATS' COMFORT

Take one raw egg, beat well and add a teaspoonful of sugar. Cats adore eggs, but do make sure that

it's properly blended; a long gloop of egg white hanging from the chin is both distracting and embarrassing.

Then there was Admiral Wallace, who only ate the middles out of stale meat pies made by a round-the-corner baker in Pimlico and dwindled to an anguished shadow when the baker moved back to Nottingham to be with his Auntie Betty who had shingles.

His owner tried everything, even baking meat pies and letting them go stale, but the Admiral only sniffed them and made discreet burying movements round them with his paw. Finally there was only one solution left, and with a heavy heart the owner bowed to the implacable will-power of his cat.

There is now a ground-floor flat for sale in Pimlico; it faces south, and the bath is done round in wicker-work.

But I also know a lot of stories about owners who insisted on giving their cats the same thing to eat week in and week out. Generally it was the same variety of tinned food bought in bulk from the cash-and-carry. There is nothing wrong with proprietary brands of cat foods, but don't use them all the time. Don't use anything all the time, because it's owners and not cats who start the food-fixation thing. Kittens brought up to eat a varied diet will continue to do so in adulthood if given the opportunity. Which is one way of ensuring that you don't have to go and live in Nottingham unless you really want to.

It isn't always realised that cats like a moist diet, but if you watch you will see that they always tackle the gravy first, lapping it from round the edge of the plate before working their way to the solid food in the middle. *Moist and warm* are the two golden rules and cats who are feeling poorly will often respond more readily to a little warm sweetened milk rather than the same stuff poured cold and hostile straight from the fridge.

Cats are dainty feeders and sometimes their damned daintiness would try the patience of a saint, but there are few pleasanter sights than that of a cat with ears pricked forward and tail aloft tripping on tiptoe to its plate, sniffing appreciatively and then settling down to eat. Just look at it — the elegant crouch, like a little fur hassock with feet, the head bobbing gently (the more a cat's head bobs the greater its enjoyment), the eyes closing dreamily. Every mouthful is properly disposed of before beginning on the next, the sound of mastication is kept to an absolute minimum, and when the last morsels have been eaten and the plate lovingly polished, the cat will rise, delicately shake its back feet and retire to a quiet place to wash its hands and face.

The whole performance is a lesson in what used to be called the Social Graces. *Go to the cat, thou clodhopper; consider her table-manners and be wise.*

Here are some more recipes calculated to improve relations between cat and owner:

DOGS' JUGULARS

Macaroni cooked in either (a) leftover gravy from the Sunday joint, or (b) stock made from half a chicken cube. Mix with an equal amount of Cats' Basic and raw minced pigs' melt, and serve warm.

BILLINGSGATE SAUNTER

The heads and tails of 1lb of sprats. (You will have eaten the rest.) Boil in a little water, strain and mash well. Mix in one tablespoonful of baby cereal such as Farex, then add enough of the liquid to make a nice little puddle of juice round the plate. Store any remaining sprats and their juice separately, as together they will set in a sullen and intractable lump which can be tiresome to deal with.

MOCK MOUSE

Cats are inordinately fond of liver, which is a good thing because it's very nourishing. The only snag is the price; even ox liver, which is the cheapest, is getting beyond a joke, but it's worth buying half a pound of it and blending it with one pound of ox or pig melt. (Ox is the big bloody one in a skin, and pigs' is the slithery, more refined-looking variety.) Simmer them together, then mince them and serve with gravy to which a little brown bread has been added.

Melt, which is the spleen of the animal, has some nutritional value but not much. Lights, (which are the lungs), have none at all, and although some cats set great store by them, it's best to serve them either in a good gravy or with some other form of meat.

And it's important to bear in mind the fact that in the ordinary wear and tear of life, it's often the cat's kidneys which first show signs of strain. There's not much that anyone can do about this, although some vets are of the opinion that the more carbohydrate a cat can be induced to eat, the longer his kidneys will stay healthy.

For all of us, however, something's got to go *ping* in the end.

Which reminds me of a cat called Matty who ate elastic bands. It took her so long to get through one that her owner concluded that it was the chewing part she most enjoyed. (A pure case of the Journey and not the Arrival.) He tried very hard to discipline Matty from her dangerous fixation, even to the point of banishing all elastic bands from the house, and it was only when his poor little cat became quite ill with frustration that he began to rethink the problem in terms of an acceptable substitute.

Matty now chews spearmint gum, but only when they are alone, and when her jaws are tired she spits it out under the chair.

To finish this chapter on a less bizarre note, here is a very fine dish suitable for special occasions. It's called BOSTON BANQUET after a family of cats who lived in a tithe barn in Boston Lincs. (not Boston Mass., although the same dish might well be a winner over there too.)

For a good blow-out for four cats you need two rabbit legs, which are simmered in a beef stock cube along with one carrot and a little raw cabbage. When cooked, take the meat off the bones and dispose of the vegetables. (Their goodness will now be in the gravy.) Add to the stew two tablespoonfuls of creamed potato which you have saved from your last night's supper, and finally stir in one tablespoonful of baked beans. This, in the words of the immortal cat book, will be *greatly appreciated*. In fact, the same thing with the addition of onion, salt and pepper and a *bouquet garni* goes down a treat with human beings too, so why not all sit down together?

2

Having Kittens

This is a process which takes from about sixty-three to sixty-five days, although it can be difficult to know when to start counting because some females are remarkably discreet about their marital affairs and regard getting pregnant as nobody's business but their own.

Others, and this includes Siamese, make an appalling song-and-dance about it. Lustfulness always seems to overtake them very unexpectedly and they rush blindly to the nearest exit screaming all-hell for a tom. Some owners can be very confused by this, like my friend in Leominster who became convinced that his cat must have eaten the packet of firelighters he had left on the kitchen table, and wrapping her in a blanket, gave her a salt water emetic. He didn't see her any more for nearly three days and when he found the firelighters in the cupboard under the sink (which is where they should have been anyway), he sat down and cried.

Sixty-one days after her return she gave birth to quadruplets, which surprised him very much.

set about eating the placenta. Don't stop her. Don't even try (like one over-zealous owner) to chop it up for her. It's all part of the process laid down millions of years ago, and scientists have now discovered that the placenta contains substances which stimulate the milk supply.

Normally the kittens will be born at intervals varying from ten to twenty minutes, and when the family is complete and the last placenta has been disposed of, the cat will set about examining her offspring at leisure; grooming them, nuzzling them and trilling encouragement as they grope blindly towards the source of nourishment. Kittens will start to suckle about half an hour after they are born.

Don't handle them yet. Content yourself with stroking their mother's head very gently while you offer your congratulations, then go away and prepare a large saucerful of Cat's Comfort for her.

And a large gin and tonic isn't a bad idea for you, either.

During the next few days she'll only leave them long enough to skip to the loo or snatch a quick meal, and although she's no longer pregnant — on the contrary, she'll look thin as an empty cushion cover — she'll need even more good food and milk during lactation. She also wants peace and quiet in which to enjoy the fruits of her labour. Almost all animals (I believe that moles are one of the exceptions), experience this overwhelming gush of love for their young, and I don't see why they shouldn't be allowed to enjoy it during the short period of rest before all the hard work begins. (I feel just as strongly about human mothers.)

As for the kittens, they are born blind and toothless, with tiny ears folded close against their skulls.

Their fragility is awesome.

During the first week they will do little but sleep and feed, their mother will keep them spotlessly clean and it will all seem very easy.

Then between seven and ten days their eyes will begin to unseal and they will become increasingly keen to try their legs. This is the time when creatures in the wild are at their most vulnerable, and their mother will probably decide that they must leave the nest for a new place of concealment.

Once again, it's a great help if you can see it her way; although she *knows* that she's living safely in a house and she *knows* that you have her kittens' welfare at heart, at such crucial times as this her fundamental instincts take over and the urge to hide her young can come close to paranoia.

Try to put up with it, because it will only last for a couple of weeks; and in any case, there's something so strangely primeval in the sight of a cat carrying a kitten in its mouth that it tends to stifle any irate questions about where the dickens it thinks it's taking it — in the bud.

So you will have kittens under cushions, kittens in the bed and kittens in the broom cupboard. Wherever you go step carefully, and above all I beseech you to sit down very carefully because one irresponsible *descent* could bring about the very tragedy your little mother cat is trying so assiduously to avoid.

At about four weeks old you can begin to think about weaning. Cows' milk is so different in composition from cats' that it often causes diarrhoea, so it's better to invest in a proprietary brand such as Sherley's *Lactol.* Some kittens will take to lapping with immediate enthusiasm while others regard the idea as ridiculous. Don't hurry them; no cat has ever

failed to lap eventually. Solid food — tiny amounts of cooked and finely minced meat and fish — is taken at the rate of six meals a day to begin with, but this should have been whittled down to two (morning and evening), by the time the kittens are five months old. As soon as they start to eat solid food they'll need a litter box. Their mother will show them how to use it and they'll take to the idea with gusto.

All this takes place during the picture postcard stage. The visual charm of kittens has been ruthlessly exploited ever since the first Victorian painted one on the lid of a chocolate box. Personally I believe that God endowed them with this special physical beauty as a means of protection against the vengefulness of humans who have just had their stockings laddered, their seedlings uprooted and their jigsaw puzzles scattered. Our last set of kittens ran up and down people's legs so much that some of them complained that it was like having acupuncture, and one lady who suffers from arthritis swore that it actually eased the pain, but I think she was probably confusing it with the relief she experienced when they stopped.

Here are two games to keep kittens amused:

SHATTER THE SHEIK

For this a newspaper is required, preferably a large Sunday one.

The newspaper must be opened and propped up on the floor in the shape of a tent. One kitten (the Sheik) will immediately dash underneath it and wait, motionless. Kitten number two will creep cautiously round the outside, then poke its paw underneath by way of opening hostilities. The paw will immediately be seized by the Sheik, who will then be leaped upon from a great height by kitten number three. The tent will be demolished, and in the uproar of tearing paper and flying bodies every effort must still be made to evict the Sheik from what remains of his property. Obviously the more kittens available, the better the sheik-shattering will be.

COLDITZ

This needs a cardboard box about two feet square. Turn it upside down and cut a doorway in either end, it adds greatly to the hazards of the game if the doorways are of different sizes: make the small one just the right size for one kitten to squeeze through. It's also a good idea to make a small hole in the bottom of the box, which of course is now the roof. As in the previous game, immediately the box is placed in position on the floor a kitten will rush in to it. He will be the P.O.W., and this time he must endeavour to escape while the other kittens (the Goons) do all within their power to prevent him. This they will do by bashing at him through either doorway and prodding him from the hole in the roof. The game has numerous variations and sometimes all the kittens will be incarcerated within Colditz together; when this happens, it's not unusual to see the box moving swiftly round the room as of its own volition.

Whatever the game — and despite their prettiness kittens always prefer those of a tough and bellicose nature — it's fairly certain that their mother will join in too, but only in an advisory capacity. Cats are incredibly good at teaching things. They are very serious and systematic about it, and a typical curriculum for a set of eight week old kittens will include all or most of the following:—

Toilet training (which includes digging, doing, covering over and patting down.)
Washing, nibbling for parasites and blow-drying.
Running, jumping, pouncing, claw-sharpening, all-in-wrestling and tree-climbing.
Mouse-detecting, fly-catching and the stalking of humans.

A remarkable cat called Urfa (I often wondered whether she was named after Urfa Kitt, but didn't like to ask), taught her kittens to sleep on the beds, and as this was technically forbidden she also taught them to smooth the creases out of the counterpanes afterwards.

Teaching is done by demonstration and explanation. Mother cats talk to their offspring practically non-stop and if you listen carefully you can soon distinguish between encouragement and command, warning and downright forbiddance. It's all done by means of chirrups and trillings and little electric bell-like noises, whereas when cats communicate with humans it's always by means of the more formal *miaow*. Only very rarely is this rule relaxed (it's much more inflexible than *tu*-ing and *vous*-ing), but the day you are greeted by a sweet gutteral whirring sound is the day when you can be said, from the cat's point of view, to have truly *arrived*. It's an honour not lightly bestowed, and cannot be won by roast chicken alone.

Kittens grow up to be cats, and the time comes when you have to make a decision about finding homes. This isn't always easy, (no kitten should leave its mother at less than eight weeks old incidentally), and if you decide to keep them all you must remember that the little females will be ready to breed at between five and seven months. Long before they swing into production however, their mother will have produced another litter, and by the end of two years you will have cats the way other people have houseflies.

And make no mistake, they will all be sunk in decadence. What at first sight seems like precocious intelligence will swiftly decline into morbidity, introspection, Baudelairean brooding and a tired acceptance of spiritual decay. They will sit in dark corners thinking about incest and child molestation, and instead of contenting themselves with the healthy extrovert's passing sniff at the catnip growing in the front border they will roll it into stealthy little cigarettes and smoke it, drawing the awful fumes deep into their lungs with a tired sigh. They won't wash. They will trip over mice with no more than a bored expletive and when they walk in the moonlight they will cast no shadow.

All of which will, I hope, make it abundantly clear that inbreeding is bad and that a line has got to be drawn somewhere.

A lady in her seventies, long widowed, received and finally accepted a proposal of marriage from an old family friend. Her grandchildren of eight and nine were heard discussing the affair. 'Is she pregnant?' demanded the first one sternly. 'Good God, no,' said the second, 'Grandpa had her spayed years ago. . .'

And so far as cats are concerned, spaying is the answer, my friends. Spaying for the women and neutering for the men. Both are simple operations, but must be carried out under anaesthetic by a competent veterinarian.

Spaying consists of removing the ovaries and uterus for which an obdominal incision is made. The vet will probably keep her in his care for the night, and she will have to return to him to have the stitches removed. The patch of hair that was shaved off will soon grow again. The removal of the male testes is even simpler, and both operations can be performed with impunity any time after the age of five months.

So — LONG LIVE CATS! — but only as many as you feel you can cope with.

3

Love, Hate and Technology

During the Eocene Period about fifty million years ago a small and lowly quadruped crept out of the prevailing murk in search of a little something. It must have found it, for it stayed around long enough to evolve by way of the splendid but now extinct Sabre-toothed Tiger into the family *Felidae*, which covers all the cat family from lions and tigers down to the cosy tabby.

The sort of cats we're talking about are *Felis Domesticus*, and it seems generally agreed that they originated in Egypt, although opinions differ when it comes to dating their arrival in Britain. Some say they were brought here with the invading armies of Julius Caesar, but there's also a theory that they arrived much earlier, being part of the luggage when the Phoenicians arrived in Cornwall to have a look at the tin mines. Whoever brought them, it's safe to assume that they came in the official capacity of Pest Officers.

Prior to this we had only the Wild Cat, the *Felis Sylvestris Grampia*, which is not to be confused with domestic cats which have become wild. The true Wild

Cat can only be found in the Highlands of Scotland; it looks like a heavily built and rather dingy tabby and is far too savage and intractable to chum up with.

To the ancient Egyptians the sun god Ra was the creator and ruler of the world. He was sometimes portrayed as a child at sunrise who grew to maturity with the day and then died as an old man at nightfall. Sometimes he had the head of a falcon or a bull, and there are some papyri pictures of him in the British Museum in which he has taken the form of a cat. He was fairly benign (as gods go), but eventually fell into senility and dribbled a lot, at which point the goddess

Nut changed herself into a cow and took him up to heaven on her back.

Ra had a wife-cum-daughter who after first being represented as a lioness-goddess, changed her image slightly and became Bast the famous cat-headed goddess. And Bast was rather a dear; extremely benevolent, she not only protected men from contageous diseases and the power of evil spirits, she also encouraged them to love music and dancing and often used to beat time with a sacred musical instrument called a *sistrum*.

Her likeness has been carved holding the *sistrum* in one hand and a small basket in the other, while at her feet sits a cluster of four rather formal-looking kittens. She is wearing a sort of 1930's dinner dress and an expression of ineffable calm.

The famous sacred cats lived in the courtyard of her temple at Bubastis, and Herodotus has left an account of the great annual festival held there. There were processions and a fair, and a lot of singing and dancing and wine-drinking but how much the cats shared in all this he doesn't say. It would be nice to think of them tucking in to *Brandade de Saumon* followed by a *Soufflé au Grand Marnier*, but I fancy that they just sat about in their gold earrings and Queen Mary chokers looking omniscient.

All cats, including the humble domestic mouser, were regarded with loving awe by the ancient Egyptians. The penalty for killing one, whether by accident or design, was instant death, and Herodotus was amazed to note that when a fire broke out the cat was rescued before either human beings or household treasures. Being Greek, he had a different set of values.

But cats didn't have it like that for long, and in

Europe during the centuries when Pagan nastiness was blended with a sort of off-Christian creepiness, they had a very bad time of it indeed. Associated with Satan and the Black Arts and blamed for everything from famine to a sore throat, no form of torture was considered bad enough for them. Cats were burnt, hung, buried alive, drowned or clubbed to death. Black cats suffered even more, and their martyrdom reached a peak during the time of intense preoccupation with witchcraft. In England a man called Matthew Hopkins appointed himself Witch Finder General and between 1645 and 1646 was responsible for the death of more than two hundred so-called witches. The majority of them were no more than harmless and confused old ladies but they were either drowned or burnt alive without mercy, along with the cats who were supposed to be their 'familiars'.

Not all church leaders fulminated against the cat, however. Both Cardinal Wolsey and Cardinal Richelieu were on intimate terms with their own special moggies, and Chateaubriand has left a memory of a little cat called Micetto, who belonged to Pope Leo XII and was carried about the Sistine Chapel in the folds of the Papal sleeve.

I have a kitten, my dear, the drollest of all creatures that ever wore a cat's skin, wrote the poet William Cowper to his cousin. *Her gambols are not to be described and would be incredible if they could . . . she is dress'd in a tortoiseshell suit and I know that you will delight in her.*

Samuel Johnson was gruffly fond of his cat Hodge and fed him on oysters, and then there was poor Christopher Smart, Johnson's scholar friend, who wrote a long tribute to his cat while incarcerated in Bedlam suffering from religious mania:

For I will consider my cat Jeoffry
For he is the servant of the living God, duly and
daily serving Him . . .

Artists have painted them, writers have written about them and Scarlatti composea a special *fugue* for their delectation. Marie Leczinska is said to have shared her bed with seven of them (simultaneously), and even Lenin and Mussolini were partial to their company, but perhaps the best eulogy of all came from the child of five, who said simply: 'I like cats because they know what I'm talking about.'

No doubt about it, they've had their ups and downs, and it's pleasant to sit by the fire on a winter evening with a drowsing cat on your lap and think how we've come out of the darkness into the light. Except that in some instances it's the blinding white light of the experimental laboratory.

What we're doing is wrong; just as wrong as it was to burn a sackful of live cats on the Midsummer Fire kindled each year in the Place de Grève in Paris, but always, belief in the necessity for the action gets us safely past any guilty concern for the pain we inflict. Then with the passing of time our theories change once again and we look back on our past behaviour with sickened incredulity.

Will we never, ever learn?

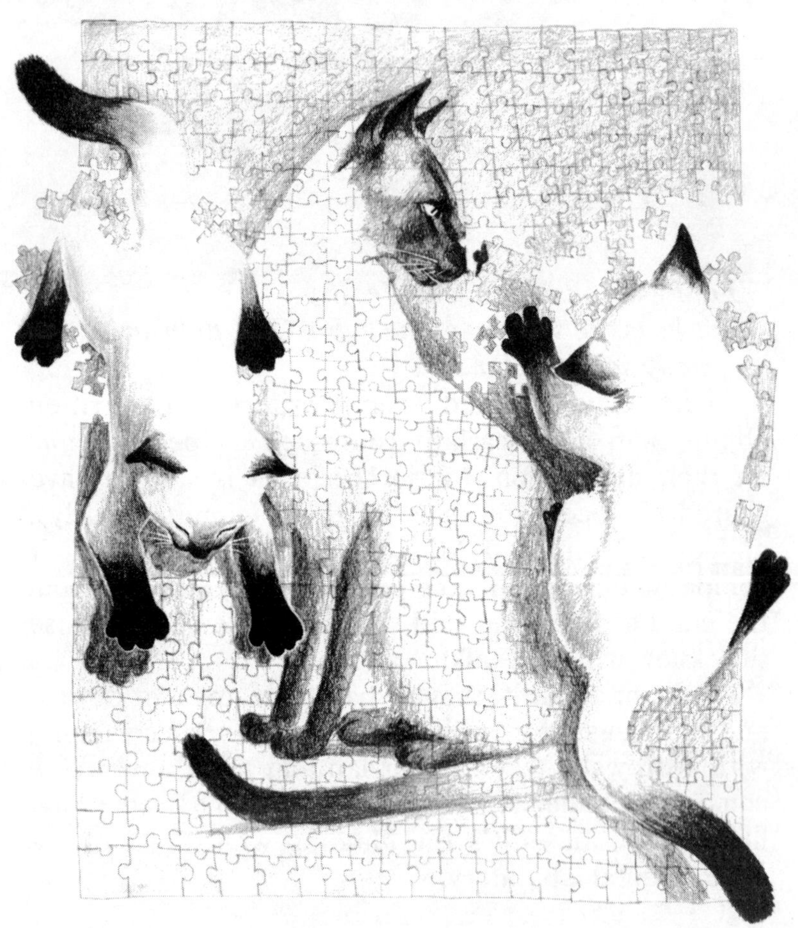

4

Cats and Humans

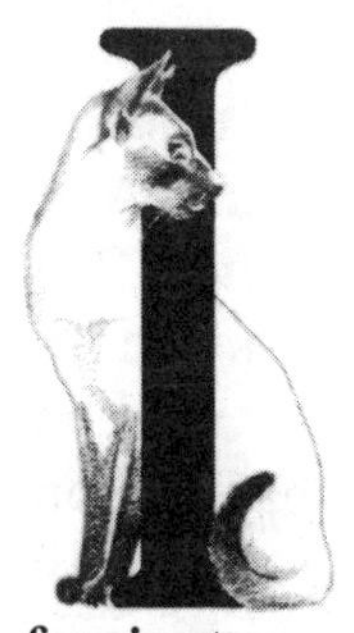

It's very interesting, living with cats. Living with any sort of animal has its interesting aspects, but with all the others it's very easy to tell upon whose foot the boot is. Introduce a brown bear or a boa constrictor into your home and you have automatically relinquished all claim to being Bigger and/or Quicker, for instance. Conversely, a lot of people adore dogs because of their shocking ability to fawn and flatter. Dogs have a masochistic love of the human boot (with the possible exception of Alsation guard dogs and a Pekinese I once knew who climbed onto a chair the better to sink its savage little fangs into the backside of an ex-European middleweight champion, but that's another story).

Cats are the only creatures who know that they are equal to human beings. Not better than, as the ancient Egyptians thought, and not less than, as most of us continue to believe. Just equal. It's a knowledge that all kittens are born with, and however much we vaccilate between one socio-philosophical theory and another, cats — who formed their opinions about most things several million years ago — see no reason for blowing their minds with questions about equality at this late date. They know precisely where they stand in their own estimation, and that's all that bothers them.

A lot of people believe that cats prefer places to people, but this simply isn't true; it's just that they prefer some people above others.

A maiden aunt of mine, for instance, lived with a black and white cat called Tissy, who helped her in the house. While my aunt dusted, Tissy would clean the crumbs from under the dining-table with her tongue, and when their daily chores were completed they would sit out in the garden with their knitting and listen to Mozart on a wind-up gramophone. And while my aunt used to click away at purl-and-plain it has to be confessed that Tissy's knitting was more of a hit-and-miss affair, for although she worked assiduously enough she rarely got beyond casting-on before becoming involved in a violent altercation with her ball of wool. She generally ended by kicking it into a flower bed and then going thankfully to sleep.

The harmony between Tissy and my aunt was marvellous to behold, and it was only when evening fell that they tended to move in slightly different circles, my aunt being fond of a game of cribbage with a friend who lived nearby while Tissy, having performed her toilette, went off to see about her mouseholes. Tissy had around fifteen to twenty mouseholes and voleholes on her territory and every one of them was given a detailed examination once every twenty-four hours.

And this beautiful existence continued until my aunt decided one Whitsun to marry her cribbage partner. He had been hinting for a long while, but she had always preferred to talk of other things until

it suddenly struck her that it might be interesting to get married and share her home with a human being as well as a cat. (She was quite firm about not going to live in *his* home because it faced the Ebenezer Chapel.)

So they married, and after a two week honeymoon in Brittany they returned home and prepared to go on living practically the same as before.

Except for Tissy. Newly released from the cattery — how she had loathed the regimentation! — she too tried to take up the old threads but found that it didn't work. The cribbage partner made far more crumbs than my aunt and had an irritating habit, hitherto unnoticed, of sucking in air through his front teeth. He also preferred military band music to Mozart.

After ten days, Tissy removed herself. She went quietly, leaving her knitting under the sofa, and although my aunt called and called she didn't respond.

Following upon a certain amount of reconnaissance, she went to live in the cribbage partner's empty house, gaining admittance through a pantry window, and there she stayed until it was sold to a retired wholesale chemist and his wife. They were very kind to Tissy and fed her on milk and cat biscuits and cod-liver oil capsules, so she stayed on, but once a week took a trip back to her old home to check the mouseholes and see how the land lay in general. Hidden in the long grass she listened for the tender sounds of Mozart but all she heard was the braying of Colonel Bogey. She noticed that my aunt, on her now rare appearances in the garden, was becoming distinctly haggard.

'That cat seems rather morose,' said the retired chemist, and cutting out two of Tissy's cod-liver oil capsules, substituted vitamin D drops.

Then one day she disappeared. They called and called and searched high and low, but there was no sign of her. 'My poor little darling's been run over,' wept the chemist's wife. 'No cat ever leaves a good home.'

And they continued to mourn until the summer afternoon when the chemist's wife, selling tickets for a village beetle drive, walked through my aunt's gate and found her sitting in the garden with Tissy. They both had their knitting, and were listening to Mozart on a wind-up gramophone. Hurt and indignant, the chemist's wife charged Tissy with perfidy and

Tissy replied with a bland stare in which there was not the slightest trace of recognition.

For you see, it wasn't Tissy who had been run over: it was my aunt's husband, who had gone up to London a few weeks previously and stepped carelessly in the path of a number 52 bus. He died on his way to hospital and left all his money to the Army Benevolent Fund.

My brother-in-law, who is very fond of cats, avers nevertheless that they are incapable of reasoning. I disagree with him, but only quietly, because I believe him to be more intelligent than I am. (He's writing a book about Swedenborg for instance, while I'm only tinkering about with this.)

But cats *can* reason. At least, mine can. It's just that their reasoning is on a slightly different plane from that of human beings. In fact, if you take the trouble to study cats' minds and the way they work, you will discover that they are extraordinarily logical creatures. One immediate example I can think of is that of the late William and Mary who would queue politely to be let out of the front door, but on seeing that it was raining outside would immediately hurry along to the kitchen door and queue there, because they saw no reason to assume that it would be raining outside both doors at the same time. After all, rain has to stop and start somewhere.

This same Mary was fond of coming up to my room for an early morning greeting. Jumping on the foot of the bed she would advance, purring, up the length of me and then peer closely into my face. This was the signal for me to wake up and start rubbing the back of her neck.

Sometimes, however, she would wake me by crying outside my window, and I would have to go down and

let her in. On these occasions I would be given a perfunctory greeting as I opened the door, then Mary would hurry on ahead of me and I would return to my room in time to see her jump on the foot of the bed and march up to the pillow with every certainty that she would still find the old familiar face lying there.

This apparent flaw in Mary's reasoning I also prefer to regard as a very sensible refusal to take anything for granted. Yes okay, I'd just been downstairs to open the door for her, but so far as Mary was concerned, how was she to know that there weren't two of me? One asleep in the bed and another separate one fluttering short-temperedly about in its nightgown? Seeing only one person at a time is hardly irrefutable proof that that's all there is of them. Particularly when you don't know how to count.

Sometimes I think that we humans would be a lot happier if only we weren't so infernally certain about everything.

One of the difficulties that domestic cats have to face is that of living a Cat-life and a Human-life simultaneously, yet we, their owners, see no reason why they shouldn't achieve an effortless balance between the two. Even more difficult, we expect them to know *when* we require a Cat-reaction as opposed to a Human-one and vice versa. I think it's asking

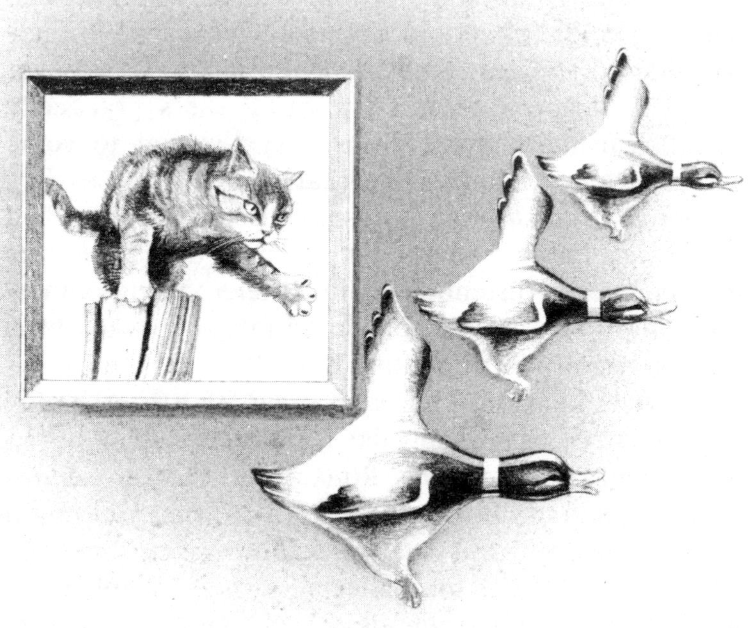

rather a lot, for example, that cats should hate mice but love birds, and that they should dig their latrines in the garden but not uproot the candytuft while doing so. (Uprooting groundsel and chickweed is again a horse of an entirely different colour.)

But despite the lure of central heating and the wall can-opener, I believe that cats' Cat Lives are still very important to them, and that being deprived of the chance to be Totally Cat for a few hours out of every twenty-four makes them sicken in their minds; this is why cats kept permanently in cages suffer from clouded perception and a chronic sense of nothingness.

It must also go part way to explaining how it is that a cat can leave the warmth of its family fireside and sit for two hours on a gatepost in a December frost without catching cold.

It's strange what a lot of people grow to look like their dogs. We all know of intellectuals who look like basset hounds, of retired colonels who resemble their wire-haired terriers, (and in all the pictures I've ever seen of Elizabeth Barrett Browning she's practically indistinguishable from Flush), but I've yet to come across anyone who looks like a cat.

Being kittenish is an accusation sometimes levelled at over-excitable women, but none of them bear the least physical resemblance to kittens, being almost unfailingly on the wrong side of forty-five with little short legs and a lot of pouting lipstick.

But I do know of a cat who grew for a short space of time to look remarkably like his owner.

The owner's name was Ronald and the cat's name was Alfonso, and Ron and Alf were on what you might call the fringe of the art world, Ron having invented a mechanical hoist for ballerinas which enabled the user to practise *pas de deux's* without the bore of having the male dancer standing about doing nothing in between lifting her up and running about with her. (The hoist, in case you're curious, was like a giant pair of forceps which operated when she pulled the ripcord attached to her person, although once it miscalculated and snatched up the tea-lady instead.) All of which has nothing whatever to do with the story of how Alf came to look like Ron.

The thing began when a woman from London University took over the ground floor flat adjacent to the one they occupied, and within a remarkably short space of time Ron had introduced himself. She was a deep-bosomed, fair-haired women who was good at practical things as well as being very good at thinking. The second time they met she asked Ron what he thought about the exaggerated imagery of the Metaphysical Poets and with great presence of mind Ron said that if she came to supper on Thursday night he would let her know. 'Splendid,' said the woman. 'And if you like, I'll bring the *hors d'oeuvres.*'

Which explains how it was that on Thursday afternoon Alf came across this bowlful of smooth cool creamy pink substance standing temporarily unattended on the table beneath the open kitchen window of Flat 4B. (The fact that Alf had no more right to be on the kitchen table of Flat 4B than he had to be on his own in Flat 4A is neither here nor there.) Let it suffice to say that cats are very fond of solitary afternoon constitutionals and if they should unexpectedly come upon a little stroke of luck during the course of one, it seems unnatural to suppose that they should not avail themselves of it.

So Alf availed himself on the kitchen table of the woman's flat, starting with a tentative lick of the edge of the bowl and working his way towards the middle.

The taste was indescribably marvellous; faintly fishy, softly seasoned and gently glutinous, it slipped down his throat almost of its own accord.

A sudden clinking sound disturbed him when he was just about half-way through. Instinctively he leaped back through the window and streaked for home, too blurred with pleasure to notice the child ambling along from the opposite direction kicking a pebble. He washed his hands and face and went to sleep on Ron's bed with the taste of forbidden fruit still sweet upon his lips.

Waking at twilight he heard a woman's voice say: 'I'm sorry it's only *oeufs mayonnaise*. Actually, I made a salmon mousse but something happened to it.' And strolling through to the sitting-room Alf saw that the lamps were glowing and that in the alcove a table had been laid for two. Laid properly, that is, with the lace cloth, a bunch of sweet peas and the butter knife. With a lift of the heart he recognised the woman from Flat 4B.

'This is Alfonso,' Ron said.

'He looks extremely well fed,' the woman said thoughtfully.

Alf watched while they ate supper and drank wine, and when they got to the cheese Ron took the woman's hand and told her that he was beastly lonely. Gently she reminded him that he had his cat, but seizing her other hand Ron said that while he was very fond of Alf it wasn't like having a close relationship with a human being of the opposite sex. The woman agreed, and looked even more thoughtfully at Alf who was sitting on the sofa thinking nostalgically about the first half of the salmon mousse he had eaten before being disturbed by the wretched child kicking a pebble. A small bead of saliva trembled at the corner of his lips.

To make conversation the woman asked Ron what he thought about the Three-Power Naval Pact that had recently been signed, but Ron didn't answer. He just sat looking at her and she saw naked longing shining in his eyes. She looked away, and encountered the eyes of Alf; now five hours since he had eaten, there was naked longing shining in his as well. It made her feel strange.

'Oh Amy,' Ron said at length. 'You have so much to give.'

The second half of a salmon mousse, for example, Alf added wordlessly.

'I thought we were going to discuss the Metaphysical Poets,' the woman said, a little helplessly.

But silence fell. The room became heavy beneath the weight of dreams and desires. Looking at Ron the woman saw that his entire countenance was ablaze with love. It made his eyes seem much bigger and his nose somehow longer. He breathed with a rasping sound. Then she looked again at Alf and saw that he too was ablaze in a similar fashion. His eyes also seemed bigger and his nose longer. Purring heavily he got down from the sofa and threw himself at her feet, clasping her ankle in his paws. And this was the precise moment Ron chose in which to seize the top half of her and bury his face in her hair.

'Oh Amy,' he cried. 'I could eat you.'

She and Ron were married in September, and for many weeks Alf continued to follow her about the kitchen in the hope that she would give him the other half of the salmon mousse. He never discovered, poor chap, that the other half had in fact been scooped up by the child that had passed him kicking the pebble.

And I only know of this because the year was 1929, the place was Maida Vale and I was the child. We

lived in Flat 4C at the time and I was always hoping that Alf and I might become best friends, but somehow we never did.

Cats can do a lot of things for people, and one of the things that people can most usefully do for cats is to *fuss* them.

Fussing is a very pleasant pastime, (some say it was invented by St. Francis of Assisi, and others by a lady called Latona Fussell who lived in Berkshire), but most human beings have to be taught by a cat how to do it.

Here, however, are a few preliminary tips to be going on with:—

First comes what is called the Offer. In this, the hand which is to be used for the fussing is extended towards the cat's nose so that the cat may smell it to make sure that it is suitable. The fingers are held open to indicate that they do not on this occasion hold a tidbit. (Anyone who has attempted to fuss a strange cat and been scratched or bitten for his pains will have almost invariably skipped this opening courtesy, thus leading the cat to suspect that it is about to be (a) dealt a blow, or (b) seized and sold to a furrier.) When however the hand has been examined the cat will smile with its eyes and give a slight nod, which is the signal to proceed.

Always start at the top of the head. With the fingers gently curved, work your way with a light scratching movement towards the back of the left ear. Linger there for a moment or two before moving slowly across to the back of the right ear. Continue scratching as before, and if you are doing it correctly the cat will press its head against your hand and close its eyes. It will purr.

When the left ear has been attended to, work the hand slowly down the neck, still scratching slowly and gently, and at this point there is a choice of direction. You may either work your way down the cat's shoulder and along the length of its spine to the root of the tail, or alternatively, slide the scratching hand round to the front and rub its chest. (Chest-rubbing must be done especially gently otherwise the cat is liable to lose its balance.) When this has been done it is a good plan to work slowly up the throat, which the cat will elevate, so that you may massage the chin and lower jaw. This last must be done with the index finger only.

If on the contrary you choose the spinal route, pressure may be increased as you near the tail. This area often seems particularly itchy — cats can suffer from dandruff, incidentally — and if you are fussing really competently the cat may even go down on its

elbows and raise its behind high in the air. The tail will be perpendicular and probably trembling slightly. The purr will assume a high raucous note.

A little conversation goes down very well as the accompaniment to fussing. The subject matter is not important — you may recite the Koran if you choose — but the correct tone of voice is essential. It should be low and melodious, even bordering on the monotonous, with occasional pauses which the cat may or may not fill with a quiet *miaow*.

It must be pointed out though, that part of the skill of fussing is the skill of knowing when to stop. However adept the fingers may be, there always comes the moment when enough is enough. To continue rubbing one spot once saturation point has been reached is a mark of insensitivity; as with everything else in life, sooner or later it's good policy to move on.

Cats are divided about stomach-rubbing. Our present ones adore it, but I have known others to be driven almost insane with rage by it; whether through fear of appearing undignified or merely because they're ticklish I have yet to discover.

But cat-fussing is a hobby I can heartily recommend, the cost in money being nil and the cost in time negligible. You don't even need your own cat because the world is full of other people's sitting on gateposts, sunning on doorsteps and reclining in the lower branches of suburban trees. They will all be pleased to be approached (in the correct manner) and when the fussing is finished they will sit down again and courteously watch you out of sight before washing the smell of your hand from their fur.

For cats can never be too careful when it comes to human beings.

5

Cats and other Cats

All animals that are normally born in litters like living together. It's only after they have become accustomed to living singly in the bosom of a loving human family that the fur can fly when another of their species is introduced. Cats know all about the torments of jealousy, and it can take months of patient coercion to get two adult strangers to settle down together.

Conversely, there's the case of Sam, the large neuter tabby who struck up a friendship with another cat (I never knew its sex), and they could often be seen in the garden sitting opposite one another with their limbs tucked under them. Sometimes they would be dozing and other times staring rather vacantly over one another's heads, but always they were surrounded by a sort of *aura* of companionship. There were children in Sam's family, and one summer Sam and his friend very unobtrusively took over the ridge tent which had been put up on the lawn, and something about their elderly-gentlemen presence made the children instinctively shy away from using it. Who would enter the Athenaeum dressed as a Red Indian?

In the house next to Sam's lived a family who had a grown up son called Douglas who liked cats (but only sensibly, in the way that one likes eating bread-and-butter or having a bath), and every now and then Douglas would find himself playing host to Sam, who would climb through the fanlight of his bedroom window in the small hours of the morning.

Douglas wasn't keen but he suffered Sam to sleep on his feet, which is where he always did. But the night came when Sam introduced his friend, both of them sliding smooth as cream through Douglas's fanlight, and the odd thing is that on this and all similar nights, the friend slept on the feet while Sam slept higher up on the chest. (Until, that is, Douglas stirred and dislodged them. After this they would sleep for a little while on Douglas's clothes, then when they were certain that peace had been restored, creep back to their former positions.)

There must have been something very special about Douglas's feet that Sam should make them the object of courteous self-sacrifice to his friend.

For every close friend that a cat may have, it will have a dozen acquaintances, and while remaining adamant in its refusal to allow them into its home, it is always keenly interested in their affairs.

Most people associate the feline habit of *marking*, i.e. releasing a small jet of urine against walls and bushes etc. with the sexual excesses of tom cats, but neutered cats often do it too. Primarily it's cats' way of marking their territorial boundaries, but I believe that it also serves as a method of passing on news. All cats go round their territory at least once a day and pay great attention to the fresh markings that have been deposited at various points, thus:

Avoid the cat from number 32: it has ringworm.
Bunty's people gave her a tin of salmon yesterday.
I caught seven mice in the toolshed.

The marking habit can be a nuisance, particularly when you're showing friends round the garden and instead of smelling *Zéphyrine Drouhin* all they can smell is cat, but on the other hand one man's poison is another man's *Patou*, and if cats could write their messages with ballpoint pens I'm perfectly sure they would do so.

So try to be sympathetic next time you pass a particularly pungent patch, and remember that in all probability it's merely proclaiming the glad tidings that:

Having two cats is double the pleasure of having only one. It's generally simplest to choose a couple of kittens from the same litter, but two strangers can be brought up together provided they're not too old and set in their ways; under three months is best.

It goes without saying that you will treat them both alike, and never be found guilty of the sin of favouritism. Cats are very sensitive to this, and in no time at all the spoilt one will have become rude, over-bearing and petulant, while the other one will be abnormally timid and stay mainly under the bed biting its nails.

But to share your home with two (or three) amiable and well-adjusted cats is not only a pleasure, it's also a lesson in How to Get on With Other Folk. A lot of people say that even a small group of cats always has a leader, but I think they are confusing them with either dogs or human beings. All the cat families I have known have been remarkable for their democratic outlook and they will take turns in bossing each other.

The bossing is rarely serious, in fact it's more likely to be the invitation to a game. A typical example of this is to see two cats sitting facing one another on the hearthrug. They sit up very straight and quite close together staring deeply into one another's eyes with their ears pressed slightly sideways, which makes them look as if they've got hats on. The staring goes on for some minutes, until one of the cats raises its paw and with a lovely airy movement taps the other one smartly on top of the head with it. This is the equivalent of throwing down the gauntlet. The other one taps back, which is a sign for the first cat to attempt to seize its opponent round the neck and lug it to the ground. This will be strenuously resisted; tails will lash, and the hats will now appear to be jammed down on their heads very firmly indeed. Ultimately the second cat will be floored, and the second phase of the game comes when both cats are lying facing on the hearthrug with their paws locked round one another and their back feet kicking one another's stomachs. Claws will be sheathed although expressions will be murderous, and the cat that can withstand the rhythmic, piston-like assault the longest is declared the winner. He will generally follow up his victory by pursuing the vanquished from the room and hitting him lightly on the bottom as he does so.

Tempers are rarely lost in such games; tails are waved and pupils of the eyes become enlarged, but this is merely an indication of the keen sportsman. You can always tell when a cat is becoming seriously upset or over-excited: it winks.

Then comes sleep. Cats tend to take their exercise in short sharp bursts (hence they're a dead loss on long walks), and exhaustion overtakes them abruptly. Yet somehow they always reserve a last little bit of energy for the preparation needed for sleep. This is mainly washing; faces and hands, privates, and then the detailed stroking down of the outer, waterproof coat (the guard hairs), until everything is arranged to its owner's satisfaction. Then the curling round in a neat snail-shape with the nose and mouth protected by the tip of the tail. (When cats are particularly exhausted, or particularly full of food, they will curl round especially tightly and press their paws against their eyes an an indication that they are Not at Home.)

Cats love to sleep together. They start off tidily enough, but as their slumber deepens they become increasingly entwined and form marvellous and intricate skeins of living fur. If you bought such a thing as a work of art it would cost you the earth.

But aesthetic reasons apart, there are many practical reasons for having cats instead of merely A Cat, and one of them is that they are far less likely to be pernickety about their food. A cat sitting down to eat in the company of its brothers and sisters is advised to fall to without wasting time wondering if it *really feels* like Billingsgate Saunter. By the time it has found out, it will be too late anyway. (Another good tip for getting a cat to eat its food, incidentally, is to put it out for the birds. Appalled by your lunacy it will rush out there and then, and mop up the lot within minutes.)

A short while ago I said that I didn't believe that cat families had leaders, but I do remember one cat that had an awful lot of *influence*. It was a rather battered old soul with only one eye, who was called Grandma. (Presumably she had started off with another name, but after years of steadily producing kittens no one could remember it.) Still, Grandma was given the respect to which her age and fecundity entitled her, being the only cat out of the resident eight that was allowed to sit on the kitchen dresser.

I spent a lot of time one summer watching Grandma with the other cats, and on first acquaintance she seemed a rather overpowering, interfering sort. Two of the other cats had kittens, and although they appeared perfectly competent to deal with them, the old girl insisted on doing all the washing and, later on, the toilet-training. Once or twice I thought I saw the mothers flush with annoyance but they didn't argue, which at the time I regarded as a bit feeble of them.

It took several weeks to recognise the heart of gold beneath the bossy exterior and to realise that it wasn't always a case of Grandma sticking her oar in. She was a skilful hunter for instance, always bringing in

rabbits and pheasants from the fields and setting them down in the barn for the other cats to share, and she was the only one of the eight who learned to manipulate the old finger-latches on the farmhouse doors. Kittens used to ask her to let them in (or out) and if there were no human beings within easy distance she would generally comply.

Because everyone had great faith in Grandma's high level of common sense no one worried unduly when she didn't turn up for supper one night. The other cats appeared equally undismayed. During the course of the next day we called her and searched round the farmyard; some of the other cats came too, but only in a benevolent, rather jokey sort of way. By supper-time that night the empty space on the corner of the dresser was beginning to get on everyone's nerves.

We'd been asleep for hours when the noise woke us; a weird hollow keening like a ghost wind sobbing at the gates of hell. It wailed on and on, this blending of unearthly voices that seemed to be coming from somewhere out in the fields. We pulled on trousers and jerseys and followed the sound, very apprehensive of what we might find.

We found the cats, all of them huddled in a tight pack round Grandma. They still kept on with their awful broken wailing and it can only have been my horrified imagination that made it sound as if they were forming consonants and fluttering little fragments of words. In the light of the torches we saw that Grandma was in a gin-trap, that she had a broken back and that she was still alive.

And this is the part that will haunt me for ever: they wouldn't let us touch her. One of the friends who was with us had had veterinary experience, and although he tried with all the skill and gentleness at his command to release her, the cats wouldn't let him, even though they knew him and normally trusted him. It just seemed as if they hated us quite savagely for intruding on their private grief.

So we had to leave. And when we went back at first light Grandma was dead and the other cats had gone.

6
Cats' Alphabet

And here to end with is a quick check list of some of the things that can harass the cat-owner — experienced and otherwise:

AGE A ten year old cat should still be fit and happy and show no sign of ageing. By fourteen or fifteen they can be said to have had a pretty good innings, although some cats can live on in to their twenties. But never let a cat suffer the misery of old-age. It's a terrible moment when you decide to ring the vet, but it should be some consolation to know that you are doing the kindest thing for your old friend. Death by injection (Nembutal) is gentle, peaceful and painless and I wouldn't mind going the same way. But not yet, not yet.

BATHING Only bath a cat if you really have to. It generally frightens them very much and normally they're quite competent to deal with the removal of mud etc. themselves. In the case of some substance which would make them ill to lick off, use a good cat shampoo and take care to keep the head well above water.

CANKER The most common ear trouble. Generally started by mange parasites which live in the ear and set up extreme irritation. The cat scratches and shakes its head, and in neglected cases the ears often have a nasty smell. You can buy proprietary brands of canker powder or lotion at the chemist's, but if it's really bad see your vet. It's a good idea to give cats' ears a gentle routine clean with a swab of cotton wool moistened with hydrogen of peroxide (10 vols.) every three months or so. But, I repeat, *gently*.

DOORS Cat-doors are a mixed blessing. While they enable the cat to come in and out without assistance they also enable other and maybe less desirable creatures to trail in and out as well. Some friends near here had a bantam hen who used to burst through the cat-door with great aplomb and lay her eggs on the kitchen windowsill.

ENTERITIS is a killer. Get the vet. Symptoms are high temperature, refusal to eat but an apparent longing for water which the cat doesn't seem capable of drinking. It will feel pain however gently you handle it, and if left without medical attention will certainly die within forty-eight hours. Enteritis is extremely infectious, and any cat thought to be suffering from it must be immediately isolated from any others. Bedding must be burnt.

To prevent all this, have your kittens immunised at three to four months and don't forget the annual booster shot. It's worth it, and in fact most catteries refuse to board cats these days unless they take their current certificates of immunisation along with them.

FLEAS (And while we're at it, LICE & NITS) Fleas are a common problem and a source of great irritation in more sense than one. Repeated scratching can break the skin and set up an infection. Although people talk about the Cat Flea as opposed to the Human Flea, they hop from one to the other quite happily. Lice are smaller than fleas but equally blood-thirsty, and it's the eggs laid by the female that are called nits. All these little creatures can be kept at bay with special veterinary products made for the job — for heaven's sake never try spraying your cat with fly-killer!

GROOMING Cats' reactions vary; some wallow in it while others see it as a form of criticism and/or interference. You certainly shouldn't need to make a big thing of it with short-haired cats, but the ones with long hair need help if they're not to look like an animated gorse thicket. A brush and comb and lots of patience is the only answer.

HAIRBALLS These form in the cats' stomach and are the result of swallowing too much loose hair when washing. They are much more common in long-haired cats and the best form of prevention is to lend a hand with the brush and comb (see above), particularly at moulting-time. Cats will often vomit swallowed hair, or it may be passed in the faeces. If a really large hairball is present and can't be shifted with a desertspoonful of olive oil you must seek professional advice because an operation may be necessary.

INFLUENZA (Feline Distemper) Another serious illness. Very like our 'flu with all its attendant miseries, i.e. aching limbs, running nose and eyes, coughing and a high temperature. It's also extremely infectious and other cats in the house will almost certainly catch it. (But dogs won't, because Canine Distemper comes from a different virus.) Treat the patient as you would hope to be treated yourself; warmth and quiet with tempting little snacks on a tray. And in the cat's case it's important to have a litter box handy so that it won't need to go out in the cold. Cats speedily die of Influenza if it's neglected, and you must remember that the virus can hang about for three months afterwards, so don't invite any strange cats or kittens in until after then.

JUDGING Sometimes people get the urge to put their cat in a Cat Show but it's a waste of time really, because they already *know* that their cat is indisputably better than anyone else's.

KILLING — AND THE LAW If someone runs over your cat you have no legal redress because, believe it or not, there are certain occasions when a cat is classed as a non-animal. This is one of them. If on the other hand someone kills, maims or wounds your cat with malicious intent, then you can sue them because the cat is (or was) your private property. But if your cat eats next-door's canary they can't sue you unless they can prove negligence on your part. On the whole though, the Law seems to regard cats as beneath its notice; there's no mention of them in the *Animals Act 1971*, and I'd think twice about getting involved in any sort of legal dispute. It could cost you plenty and get you nowhere.

LOST CATS You can go to your local police station and *Furnish a description*, but I don't hold out much hope; most of the time the police have got their hands full with human beings. You could try the local branch of the R.S.P.C.A., who will in turn put you in touch with the nearest Cats' Protection League. Other than this, ask neighbours to keep a look out, keep on calling your cats' name around his recognised haunts, and when he turns up again give him a huge meal and a lot of fussing.

He may have gone off because he was suffering from self-doubt.

MOVING HOUSE is one of the commonest causes of cats getting lost. Keep the cat locked up while the removal men are at work, and if it's possible for it to travel to the new home in your company, let it do so. But in any case it must be in a travelling basket or box which is large enough to accommodate both the cat and his own familiar cushion or woolly. It must also be well endowed with air-holes and secure against possible escape — unlike dogs, cats go completely to pieces when faced with unfamiliar surroundings and it's a terrible business trying to recapture them. When you reach your new home keep the cat in for several days (this will entail the temporary use of a litter box), and give it ample opportunity to explore the house. And although you're very busy, try to give it a bit of extra fussing. The reason why cats sometimes attempt to go back to their old homes is because they're looking for the dear old peaceful pre-removal You; contrary to popular theory, they don't give a damn about the house itself.

NEW CATS AND KITTENS A lot of the above applies here, too. Go easy with the newcomer. Encourage it to explore its new home and make sure that it knows where to find its own sleeping accommodation, its own toilet facilities and its own food bowl. Feed it at regular intervals. A sense of continuity is a great comfort to any animal trying to settle itself in fresh surroundings. Talk to it; move about quietly and don't make it jump.

OUT-AT-WORK-ALL-DAY-OWNERS Some people are consumed with guilt because they have an animal and are out at work all day. If it's a cat, I don't think they need worry themselves unduly provided they've left it with adequate food and water and either a litter box or a means of getting in and out of doors. Dogs, I believe, do suffer from loneliness, but cats seem reasonably happy to sit in solitude and think. Don't stint the fussing when you get home, though.

POISONS Unless they're starving, cats are too fussy about food to be easily poisoned. The greatest hazard lies in eating rats and mice which have been poisoned. It also pays to keep a sharp eye on the ingredients listed on the containers of horticultural goods, such as arsenic (in some weedkillers), sulphate of ammonia, and of course D.D.T. Acute vomiting and probably diarrhoea are the first symptoms, and these can lead to convulsions, insanity, paralysis and all sorts of horrifying things. If poisoning is suspected, don't mess about with home-made emetics — get the poor creature to a vet with all speed.

QUARANTINE The law about this has been hammered home good and hard by H.M. Government in recent years, but it does no harm for J. Gardiner to add her little bit. All animals brought into this country from abroad MUST undergo six months' isolation in quarantine in licensed veterinary premises, where they will be given a double vaccination with an anti-rabies vaccine. Try (from soft-heartedness or any other reason) to side-step the law and you face imprisonment. You also put other people's pets at risk because the authorities have made it quite clear that they will not hesitate to destroy cats and dogs etc. within any given area should an outbreak of rabies occur. As for . . .

RABIES itself, it's a notifiable disease and a killer. Symptoms in the animal are violent and uncoordinated movement, madness and foaming at the mouth. It becomes paralysed and dies in great pain within a few days. A bite from an infected animal can be fatal to humans, and it's not a nice way to go.

STINGS Cats are fond of examining bees and wasps, often to their detriment. Wasps don't leave their stings behind, but bees do. Remove sting (which won't be easy!) and in either case apply a little antihistimine cream.

TEMPERATURE A cat's temperature can be taken with an ordinary clinical thermometer and should normally be around 38.9°(c). It's usually taken in the rectum — and much more neatly by a vet than a nervous amateur.

UNLOVED CATS often leave home and are not always successful in finding a new one. Living rough, whether in town or country, takes its toll of them before long. They become thin, flea-bitten and worm-ridden. They pick up any virus that's going, but it's amazing how long a dying cat can continue to drag itself around. Please, if you come across one like this, ring for the R.S.P.C.A. There's always a local branch, and the inspector will arrive within a short space of time and quickly and expertly do whatever is best and most merciful for the cat. He won't charge you a fee, but a voluntary donation to the Society's funds would be more than welcome.

And while we're on the subject of the R.S.P.C.A., never be afraid to ask for their advice about anything relating to the welfare of cats or other animals. They are marvellous suppliers of free leaflets on practically every aspect of pet-care and they also work in close conjunction with the Cats' Protection League, another organisation whose praises are insufficiently sung.

VET — AND WHEN TO CALL HIM This is always a tricky one. From my experience cats are very hardy creatures, but once they become ill they tend to go downhill very rapidly. A high temperature, running eyes and nose, vomiting, acute diarrhoea, and pains in the abdomen are all symptoms I would take seriously. In the case of a cat that has been run over handle it as little as possible and protect yourself with thick gloves. Lay it gently in a big flat box and get it to the vet as soon as you can. But for things like minor cuts, stings and abrasions, have a heart — particularly on a Sunday!

WORMS — TAPE AND ROUND Even the most distinguished cat is at sometime or another a martyr to worms. Roundworms are the ones that affect kittens, (the eggs can be present in their mother's milk), and if neglected can lead to rickets and anaemia. Grown up cats suffer from roundworms and also tapeworms, and the main symptoms of having either or both are unsatisfied hunger, thinness and a poor coat. Cats perpetually infested can also suffer from vomiting and diarrhoea and will become weak and sickly and a prey to any virus going the rounds. Worm pills are the answer. Healthy kittens should always be wormed at six weeks and then again at eight; be accurate with the dosage recommended on the packet. Adult cats should receive similar treatment whenever worms are seen either in the faeces or on the fur around the tail region. Sherley's make a very good combined pill for both sorts of worms; its called the *Multi-Wormer for Cats* and I recommend it.

X-RAYS If your vet suspects that there may be reason for having one, he will arrange it. It may entail giving the cat an anaesthetic in order to keep it still.

YOWLING Cats pop-singing. Lovely for them, but a bit of an acquired taste for others — particularly in the middle of the night.

ZOIATRIA The up-market name for your vet's surgery. It comes from the Greek *zoion* meaning animal and *iatreia* meaning healing.

And having imparted this final gem it only remains for me to say good-bye, and to thank you for the pleasure of your company.